Ships of the Great Lakes, A Pictorial History

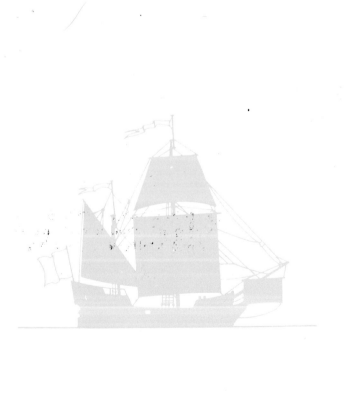

Ships of the Great Lakes, A Pictorial History

Paintings by Karl Kuttruff

Introduction by Robert E. Lee

Captions by David T. Glick

Wayne State University Press   *Detroit, 1976*

Library of Congress Cataloging in Publication Data
Kuttruff, Karl, 1941-
    Ships of the Great Lakes.
    1.   Ships—Pictorial works.   I.   Title.
VM307.K87   386'.22'0977   76-10383
ISBN 0-8143-1564-X

    *Grateful acknowledgment is made to the Board of
Directors, Great Lakes Maritime Institute, for financial
assistance in the publication of this volume.*

Contents

Acknowledgments

The Dossin Great Lakes Museum is proud to be part of the Bicentennial volume *Ships of the Great Lakes, A Pictorial History* and will benefit greatly for years to come from the generosity of the Detroit Historical Society Guild in providing a special grant to commission the paintings reproduced here, which will become part of the Museum's permanent collections. We wish also to express appreciation to the Board of Directors of the Great Lakes Maritime Institute for their willingness to commit funds to the full extent of the organization's limited means in partly underwriting publication costs, thus helping to realize Robert E. Lee's original conception of the book as a Bicentennial project.

The artist would have found it next to impossible to complete the paintings without the assistance of many persons and groups in the form of encouragement and of generosity in supplying data, drawings, and photographs. Thanks are especially due to Dr. David Armour and the Mackinac Island State Park Commission; Charles Brewer; Gordon Bugbee; Frank Crevier; William Keller; William Lundy; Emory Massman; Edward Middleton; Arthur O'Hara and the Great Lakes Historical Society; Gordon Potter; Ruth Revels and the Milwaukee Public Library; Gavin Sproul and the American Shipbuilding Company; Ken Thro; and Harry Wolf. The artist also owes a debt to the late Captain Frank E. Hamilton for whetting his interest in Great Lakes maritime history.

Grateful acknowledgment is made to the Reverend Edward J. Dowling, S.J. and Arthur M. Woodford for their valuable assistance with research and writing.

Finally, to the staff of Wayne State University Press we cannot completely express our appreciation. Entering into this project we were complete novices, knowing only that we wanted to get out a book, but knowing nothing of the many dangers in shoal waters that awaited us. Richard Kinney expertly piloted us through these treacherous channels. The enthusiasm of Frank B. Ware and Robert Eskola from the very beginning convinced us—and we think the Wayne State University Press—that the idea we had was a good one.

Karl Kuttruff

Robert E. Lee

David T. Glick

Introduction

Robert E. Lee

The Battle of Lexington and Concord, joined in April 1775, began the adventure in New World history to be marked in 1976 as the American Bicentennial.

Almost a century earlier, at a site believed to be the present La Salle, New York, René Robert Cavelier, Sieur de La Salle laid the keel of his ship, *Le Griffon,* which we know as the *Griffin*. Historians do not agree on her dimensions; she was either of 45 or 60 tons burden, and a barque. Completed in 1679, she was to mark the first of many "new eras" in Great Lakes commerce. Ironically, this first ship on the Lakes would become the Lakes' first "Flying Dutchman." She disappeared without a trace on the return leg of her first trip and was never heard from again; to this day her fate remains an enigma to historians.

Although she was the Lakes' first sailing ship, the *Griffin* did not introduce commerce to the Lakes. For centuries the inland waterways had provided avenues of trade and communication, first for the Indian nations, and later for the French. One might wonder why it took so long for the ingenious French to arrive at the point of building a ship for the Lakes. Lake Huron had first been viewed by the Recollect friar Le Caron in 1615. Later the same year, Champlain saw both Lakes Huron and Ontario. In 1629 Étienne Brulé explored Lake Superior, 1634 brought Jean Nicolet into Lake Michigan, and Lake Erie was probably first seen by Joliet in 1669. The Lakes had been known to the French for more than sixty years when La Salle set out to beat his way around to Green Bay and establish commerce by ship in waters previously floating nothing bigger than a canoe.

The lucrative fur trade provided the base for French interest in the area. Forts were constructed to insure the security of this commerce, two more important of these being at Mackinac and Detroit. Why the French failed to build a replacement for the *Griffin* is thus difficult to understand.

It remained for the British arrival on the Great Lakes to signal the next advance in Lakes shipbuilding. By 1760 the British were well entrenched in the area and had established themselves at Detroit, but not without bitter opposition from the Indians. Lake Erie, purview of the great Iroquois Five Nations, had been broached by the British only with the help of vessels able to maintain a supply of necessities to the small community at Detroit. Thus, military need dictated the construction of ships to carry supplies and to run the Indian blockades. Two such vessels were the *Beaver* and *Gladwin,* both built in 1760 at Navy Island on the Niagara River.

It was 1769 before Detroit saw its first locally built vessel, the *Enterprise*. Virtually no information on this ship survives, leading one to believe that she may well have been an illegal vessel, unsanctioned by the "Provincial Marine," the agency controlling all ships built in Canada West. The regulations, formulated by Governor Sir Frederick Haldimand, were intended to assure that ships built within the region were built only for the good of the Crown. The result was that very little private shipbuilding was done until 1816.

One notable exception was the sloop *Welcome,* constructed in 1775 at Fort Michilimackinac by John Askin. A frontier trader, Askin used the single-masted, 45-ton vessel to carry merchandise and trade goods between Michilimackinac and Detroit. She was an armed vessel, boasting two swivel guns and two blunderbusses, and carried a crew of eight. In June of 1779, Major Arent Schuyler De Peyster, commandant at Michilimackinac, purchased the vessel for the British government for military service, and her crew was increased to twelve, plus twelve soldiers. In 1781 she was lost in a storm with all her crew and provisions.

In 1789, Leith & Shepherd, commission agents at Detroit,

together, it is believed, with Forsyth & Richardson, had a ship launched into the Rouge River. This vessel, the *Nancy,* was one hundred tons, 79 feet long, and had a 23-foot beam. She was the first ship *provably* built at Detroit, about which anything is really known. She served as a merchant vessel between Fort Erie, Mackinac, and Detroit until pressed into military service during the War of 1812. Caught on Lake Huron by the U. S. Fleet at Nottawasaga Bay, she came under the guns of the post and was sunk.

The War of 1812 focused national attention upon the Lakes. The area had passed from the French to British rule, the American Revolution had ended in victory for the colonists, yet through it all the Lakes had been largely unaffected. The question thus arises why we celebrate a Bicentennial in these parts while talking of events of only about 150 years ago. An answer is that although the peace following the Revolution awarded this territory to the new United States, in title, not much could be done to occupy the new land until after another war (1812). It remained for Commodore Perry's famous message, "We have met the enemy and they are ours," to fire up national imagination and patriotic pride in the lately ceded Lakes territory as American.

Over the 1812–13 winter season, a fleet of ships were built at Presque Isle (now Erie, Pennsylvania) with which Perry was to engage the British fleet. Among these were two twenty-gun brigs, *Lawrence* and *Niagara;* Perry selected the former as his flagship. Once in battle, the *Lawrence* fared badly and Perry found it necessary to transfer his command to the fresher *Niagara.* Being the ship of victory the *Niagara* has retained her fame, while the *Lawrence* has undeservedly been given short shrift in history—enough reason to include the latter in this work.

With "Mr. Madison's War" out of the way, and with the boundaries established in the Treaty of 1783 confirmed, settlement began in earnest and brought with it the potential for a boom in commerce. Sailing ships were soon being built in a dozen or more places around the Lakes. They formed the beginnings of a merchant sailing fleet that would hold sway for three or more decades before anyone would seriously consider a replacement for mast and sail. Men of vision were convinced that steam power would change all this, however. In 1809 the *Accomodation,* a steamboat, made a trip from Montreal to Quebec City, hardly a benchmark in Great Lakes history, but at least a beginning. The 1816–17 winter saw two launchings of ships that would join the sixty-odd sailing vessels on Lake Ontario. The *Ontario* and the *Frontenac,* one American, one Canadian, would introduce steam propulsion to the Lakes, for the first time testing the new power against water with wind and wave. All previous tests had been in rivers with relatively calm waters. These events did not go unnoticed above the Niagara Falls.

During the winter of 1817–18 a company was formed to construct a steamboat. The engine was to be built by Robert McQueen and the hull by Noah Brown. Early in 1818 the keel was laid at the mouth of Scajaquada creek, on May 28 the vessel took to the water, and on August 22, 1818, she set out on her maiden voyage. The *Walk-in-the-Water* brought a new era of commerce to Lake Erie and Detroit. A century-and-a-half later, the first thousand-foot vessel would, comparatively speaking, cause no more excitement.

As portages gave way to canals that opened the interior to settlement, so log huts gave way to fine houses. Hundreds of small communities with unimproved harbors now needed lumber. So came the lumber schooners of shallow draft and sky-high deck loads fresh from virgin forests. An industrial revolution created a need for ores at one end of the Lakes and for coal and stone at the other; to carry these heavy cargoes a different kind of ship was needed. The forerunner of the bulk freighter came into being. Harbors were deepened, unloading and loading methods improved with experience, and ship design changed to meet the opportunities presented.

As the small communities became cities, the need to keep them supplied with goods brought about the peddler boats, and as the people of these cities longed to escape, excursion and overnight boats came into their own. A few people were making great fortunes, too great to permit them to mingle with the common folk on excursion boats. Rich men built luxurious yachts; one of them even bought a Great Lakes passenger steamer, the S.S. *United States,* and had it made bigger to qualify as his private yacht.

As the automobile came onto the scene, Henry Ford built a giant plant at River Rouge, where once primitive adzes had trimmed timbers to build the *Nancy.* To supply that great plant with iron ore, Ford built two bulk freighters and named them for his grandsons. Soon another company would adapt the older bulk freighters to carry finished automobiles away from the Detroit plants to customers across the Lakes.

Change is constant. Just as the simple canals replacing the early portages grew to admit modern vessels, recent enlargement of locks at Sault Ste Marie, Michigan, made possible another "new era" with introduction of the Lakes' first thousand-foot ship, the *Stewart J. Cort.* One of the two ships Ford built a half-century earlier was recently rebuilt into a self-unloader; the *Henry Ford II* is now even more efficient than when it was new.

This account touches only briefly the imposing series of events that have shaped the development of ships and shipping upon the Great Lakes, but it should be sufficient reason to explain why the Board of Directors of the Great Lakes

Maritime Institute made the decision to present a pictorial history as their contribution to the spirit of the American Bicentennial. In those years we have counted as a nation, and for years before, many ships have crossed the Lakes, navigated rivers, and put in at forts, villages, cities, and now megalopolitan centers. A record of these ships should exist, to be seen and enjoyed, then passed on to future generations that they too may know from whence we came.

No one, of course, really knows what the earliest Lakes vessels looked like, and any rendering has to be based on the best guesses of informed persons. Early shipbuilders brought their skills with them from France and England. Ships were built by "rule of thumb" without benefit of plans. Hulls were laid out on the spot, with the master carpenter dictating "a little more here; a little less there" until a ship evolved. If that ship's design was good, it was copied by other shipbuilders. Today, anyone knowing the rudiments of hull design and sail plan, and given basic dimensions, could with reasonable accuracy reconstruct what the ship probably looked like. So, in a museum model, or in a painting, allowance must be made for the possibility that the prototype wasn't exactly as depicted, and that the replica is, at best, based upon the combination of all the available best guesses.

As American commerce grew and prospered, ship owners began to commission painters to produce portraits of their ships—whether through a sense of history or through pride of ownership is open to conjecture. The practice came late to the Lakes, however, although such paintings had become fairly commonplace on the Atlantic coast by 1800. Unfortunately, some of the early efforts fall far short of accuracy. One glaring example is in a painting of Detroit in 1820 by George Washington Whistler. Even though Whistler, an engineer, had actually seen the *Walk-in-the-Water,* his view of her in that painting is of a vessel that would surely have capsized immediately on being set afloat. Other views of Detroit in 1794 and 1837 are probably more accurate, however, in depicting the vessels in the river.

With the opening of the Erie Canal in 1825 and the resulting influx of immigration into the Lakes area, advertising artists began to make detailed and accurate pictures of what ships looked like. Chromolithography was used in preparing broadside views calculated to generate traffic for the ship depicted. Perhaps some slight exaggeration crept into the efforts of the artists in an attempt to make their vessel look much better, or larger, than the competition's. But this was usually accomplished by means of comparative scale; other ships in the picture would be drawn smaller than they were, for instance, and in the main the ship was accurately rendered. Ship portraiture was popular until the early 1900s, as proud owners sought to memorialize their vessels in offices and on ticket agents' walls. Fortunately, most of these paintings by such artists as Robert Hopkin, Seth Whipple and Howard Sprague have survived in museum and private collections, often to provide the only evidence available of a vessel's appearance.

Ship portraits went out of fashion with the advent of the photograph. As Mr. Daguerre's images on silver gave way, first to the wet and dry plate processes, then to George Eastman's box camera that anybody could operate, ship pictures became commonplace. Something, we fear, was lost in the transition. However, if the photograph fails to match the painting in artistic value, it is still a peerless research tool and historical record. Historians today give thanks to little-known photographers who thought to record a passing vessel, as well as to the many owners driven by vanity to have images of their ships committed to canvas. Without both sources, upon which Karl Kuttruff drew extensively, many of the paintings presented

in this volume would lack the pictorial and technical accuracy we know them to have.

The selection of subjects for this book was initially based upon those vessels represented in the excellent collection of models at the Dossin Great Lakes Museum in Detroit. Where ships in this volume are not from that collection it is either for the reason that the ship presented here was felt to be a better representative of its type, or because the Museum's collection lacked the particular vessel.

An effort has been made to show all of the important types of vessels in the technical development of the Great Lakes ship; vessels with one, two, three, four, or five masts; primitive sidewheeler, early "propellor," modern motor vessel; wood hull, iron hull, steel hull, etc.* Where a unique vessel existed it was used to illustrate a type, or it was included merely for its uniqueness. A case in point is the U.S.S. *Michigan,* first iron warship, or the *Lansdowne,* not just a railroad car ferry but the last commercial sidewheeler on the Lakes at the time of her retirement.

These ships will tell a separate story of the years of our Bicentennial. They speak of how the area grew and how its needs changed from a simple economy based upon beaver pelts carried in canoes to a computerized commerce employing great ships navigated by sets of transistorized instruments undreamed of as recently as a generation ago.

---

* Ship dimensions are included in the captions. Length is given in perpendiculars unless overall length is specified.

1. *Le Griffon* (Barque)

The first large vessel to sail upon the upper Great Lakes
was the barque *Le Griffon* (*Griffin*), which was built on the
Niagara River in 1679 by a French expedition led by René
Robert Cavelier, Sieur de La Salle. Contemporary accounts
record that she was about 60 feet long overall, with a beam
of 16 feet and depth of 7 feet, measuring between 45 and 60
tons. She disappeared with all hands in September 1679, while
returning to Lake Erie from her maiden voyage to Green Bay.
Thus she became the first of a long list of mystery ships of
the Great Lakes.

2. *Welcome* (Sloop)

Built in 1775 at Fort Michimilimackinac, Michigan, for
John Askin, the sloop *Welcome* was taken over by the
British Royal Navy during the American Revolution.
Constructed of white pine, she was 55 feet long overall with
a beam of 16 feet, depth of 7 feet, and measured 45 tons. She
disappeared in a storm on Lake Huron in 1781. America's
Bicentennial Year finds a replica of *Welcome* being constructed
at Mackinaw City at approximately the same site upon
which the original was built.

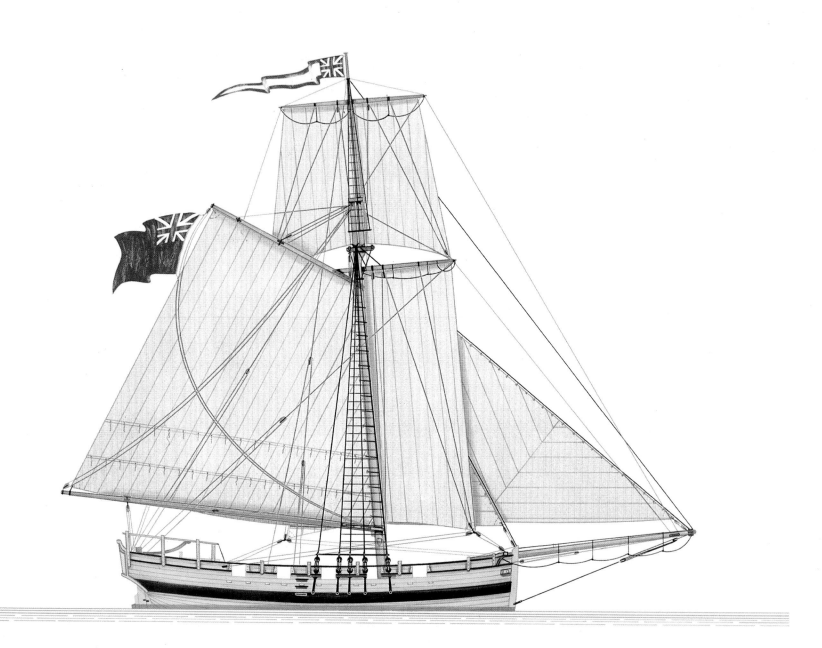

3. *Nancy* (Schooner)

The topsail schooner *Nancy* was constructed of oak and red cedar at Detroit in 1789 for John Richardson and others of Montreal for use in the fur trade. When the British Royal Navy took her over during the War of 1812 she became H.M.S. *Nancy*. She was burned in the Nottawasaga River on August 14, 1814, during an attack by United States forces. In the 1920s her bones were uncovered, and later a marine museum was built around them. She was 79 feet long, with a 23-foot beam and a depth of 8 feet.

4. U.S.S. *Lawrence*   (Brig)

U.S.S. *Lawrence* was Commodore Oliver H. Perry's flagship. This brig was built in 1813 at Presque Isle (Erie), Pennsylvania. Of 480 tons, she was 118 feet long, with a beam of 30 feet and depth of 9 feet, and mounted two 12-pound long guns and eighteen 32-pound short guns. Early in the battle of Lake Erie on September 10, 1813, she was badly damaged and Perry transferred his flag to the U.S.S. *Niagara*. However, after the battle, he returned to the decks of the *Lawrence* to receive the British surrender and pen his famous message of victory. Following the War of 1812 the *Lawrence* was scuttled in Misery Bay at Erie. Her bones were dug up and sent to Philadelphia for the Centennial Exposition of 1876 where they were cut up and sold for souvenirs. What remnants remained were destroyed in a fire.

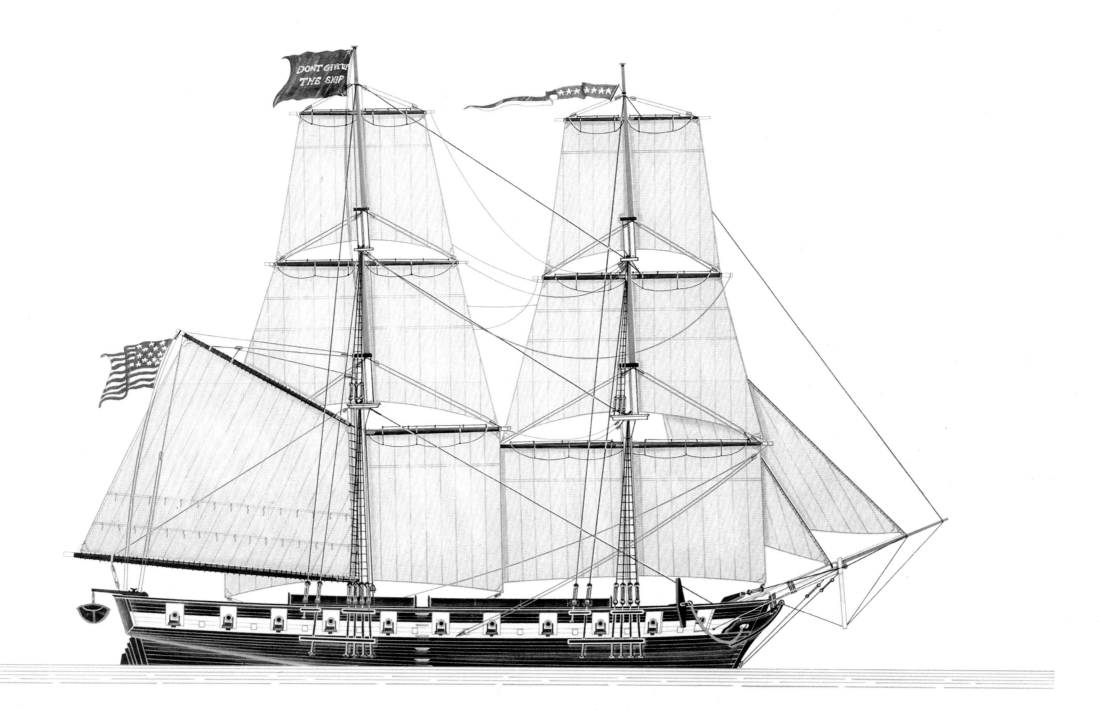

5. *Walk-in-the-Water* (Steamer)

When *Walk-in-the-Water's* 135-foot hull slid into the waters of the Niagara River on May 28, 1818, the age of steam arrived on the upper Lakes. She was a slender craft with a beam of 32 feet and depth of 8.5 feet. Her short life ended when she was stranded near Buffalo on November 1, 1821. However, her vertical cross-head engine was salvaged to sail again in the *Superior* of 1822.

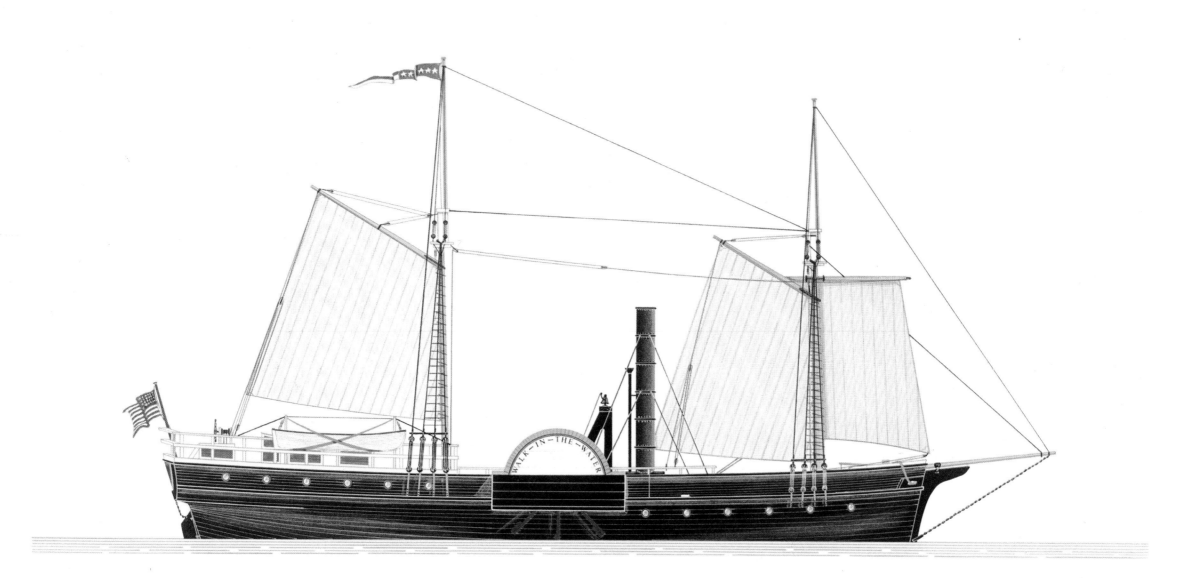

6. *Michigan* (Steamer)

When the sidewheel passenger steamer *Michigan* was launched
at Detroit in 1833 she was the largest steamboat on the Lakes,
145 feet long, with a beam of 29 feet and depth of 11 feet.
Her owner, Oliver Newberry, also saw to it that she was one
of the most luxurious. Although her usual route was from
Buffalo to Detroit, it is recorded that once each summer she
ran a special excursion to Lake Michigan, which in those days
was mostly wilderness. She thus could qualify as the first of
a long list of excursion steamers on the Lakes. By 1847
Michigan was obsolete and was laid up, although she was not
actually broken up until about 1854.

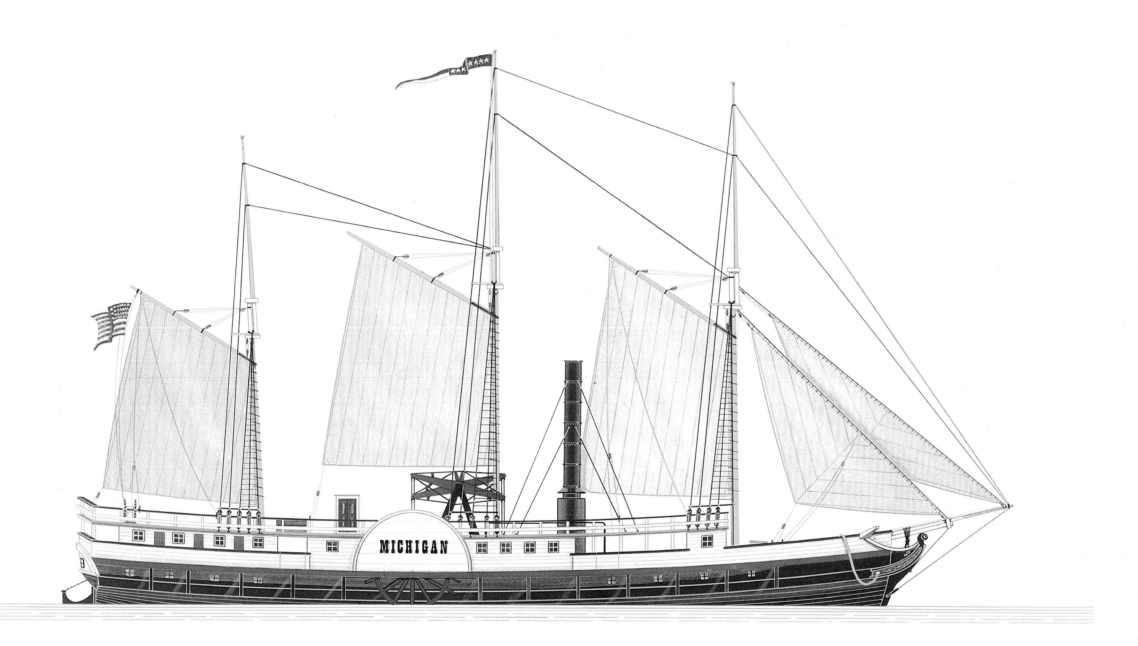

7. *Vandalia*   (Steamer)

The little 138-ton *Vandalia* was the first steamer on the Great Lakes to be driven by a screw propeller. Built of wood by Sylvester Doolittle at Oswego, New York, in 1841, the *Vandalia's* engine acting directly upon the propeller shaft saved a great deal of space and foretold the eventual demise of the sidewheel steamer. She was only 91 feet long, with a 20.17-foot beam and depth of 8.25 feet, but her shadow still looms large upon the Lakes.

8. U.S.S. *Michigan* (Gunboat)

Among the famous firsts of the Great Lakes is the United States Navy's first iron warship, the U.S.S. *Michigan* of 1844. Her parts were built in Pittsburgh by Stackhouse and Tomlinson and moved by wagon to Erie, where they were assembled. She was 163.3 feet long, with a beam of 27.1 feet, and depth of 9 feet. Although limited by treaty to one gun, the *Michigan* played her role well. Among her adventures were the Beaver Island incident involving "King" Strand and the Confederate plot to free the prisoners held on Johnson's Island during the Civil War. In 1905, when the Navy needed her name for a new seagoing battleship, she was renamed U.S.S. *Wolverine* but continued to serve both the Navy and the Pennsylvania Naval Militia until engine failure caused her to be laid up in Misery Bay, Erie, in 1923. In 1949, efforts to preserve this historic vessel having failed, she was cut up for scrap. However, at Erie her cutwater has been preserved as a monument to this real pioneer.

9. *May Flower* (Steamer)

Built for the Michigan Central Railroad by J. Lupton at
Detroit in 1849, the sidewheeler *May Flower*, 288 feet long,
with 35.5-foot beam and 13.5-foot depth, was a true palace
steamer complete with twelve bridal chambers. She was also
known for her speed, which was due at least in part to her
72-inch vertical beam engine, built by Hogg & Delamater in
New York City. Hers was a short life, which ended when she
stranded upon Point Pelee, Lake Erie, on November 20, 1854.

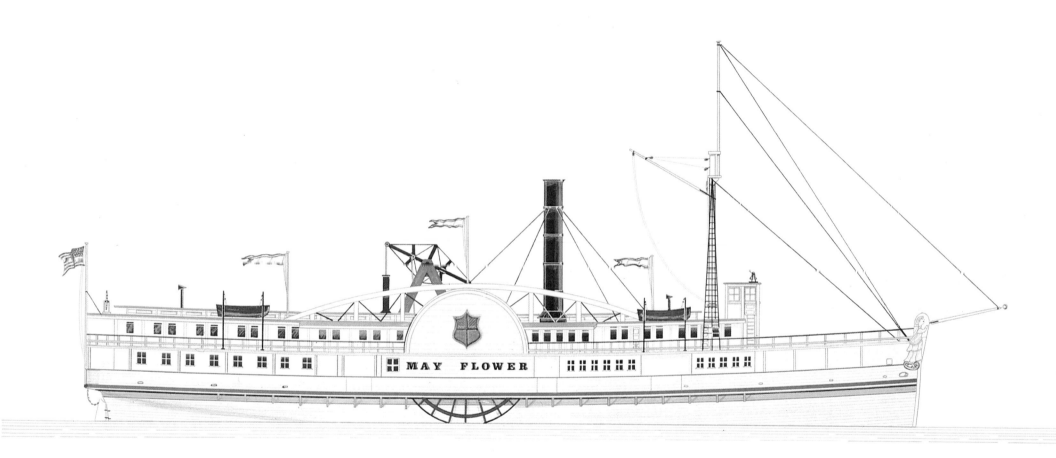

10. Mackinaw Boat   (type)

These small vessels, usually about 35 feet in overall length, with a beam of 8 feet and depth of 3 feet, on the average, developed on the Canadian side of Lake Huron and on Georgian Bay around 1850 and were extensively used in the fishing industry until the advent of powered boats. The traditional Mackinaw was double ended, cat rigged, with no bowsprit or jib, and a full-frame, clinker built hull with a centerboard. The foresail was larger than the aftersail and both were gaff rigged. Years of adaptation on the Lakes, however, led to many variations. Although showing European influence in their design, Mackinaw boats were unique to the Upper Lakes.

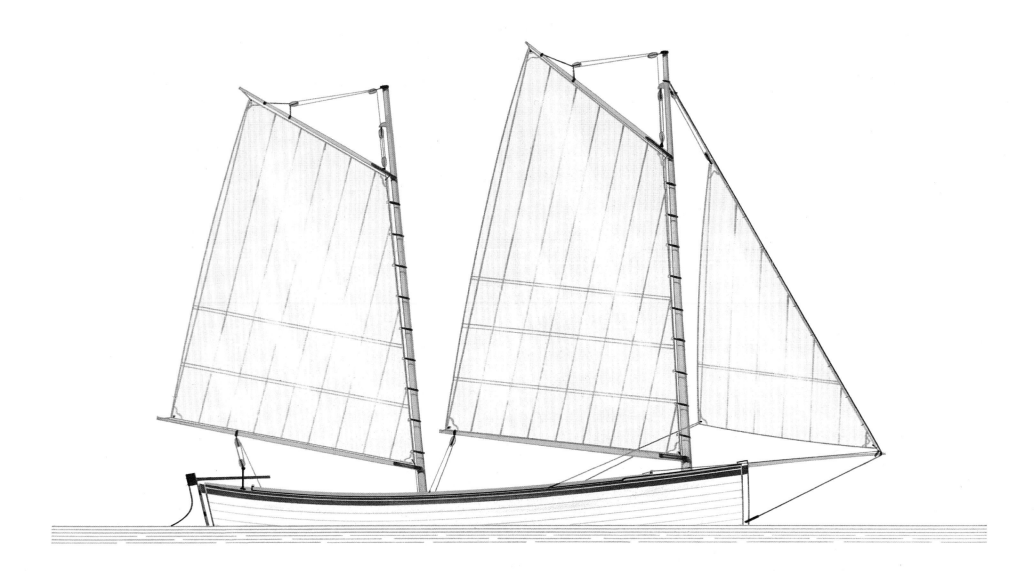

11. *Challenge* (Schooner)

With *Challenge* of 1852 Manitowoc shipbuilder William Bates began the evolution of the Lakes' most handsome sailing hull design, which some believe to be a condensed version of America's famous seagoing clipper ship. Although the two-masted *Challenge* was only 87 feet long, with a 22.6-foot beam and depth of 7 feet, her design continued to influence Lakes vessels until the end of the age of sail.

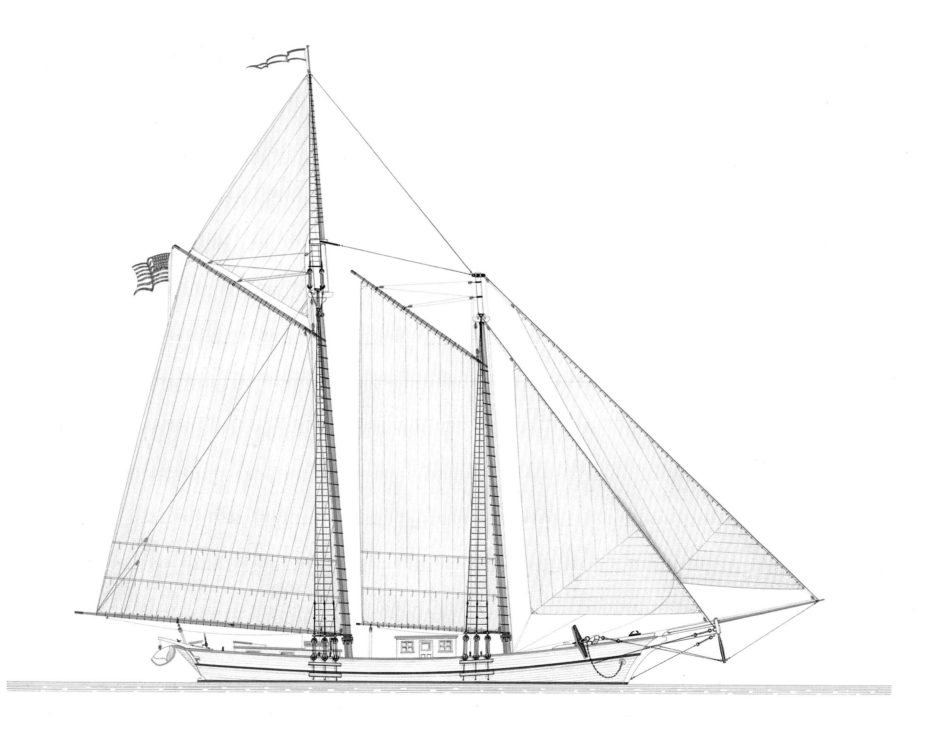

12. *Milton* (Scow-Schooner)

Scow-schooners were built on the Great Lakes by the hundreds
in the nineteenth Century. They were easy and inexpensive
to build and could navigate in very shallow water. *Milton,*
built at Milwaukee in 1867, was typical of her breed. She was
132.4 feet long, with a beam of 29.2 feet, depth of 8.7 feet, and
measured 234 tons. Her days ended when she was blown
ashore near Two Rivers, Wisconsin, in 1885.

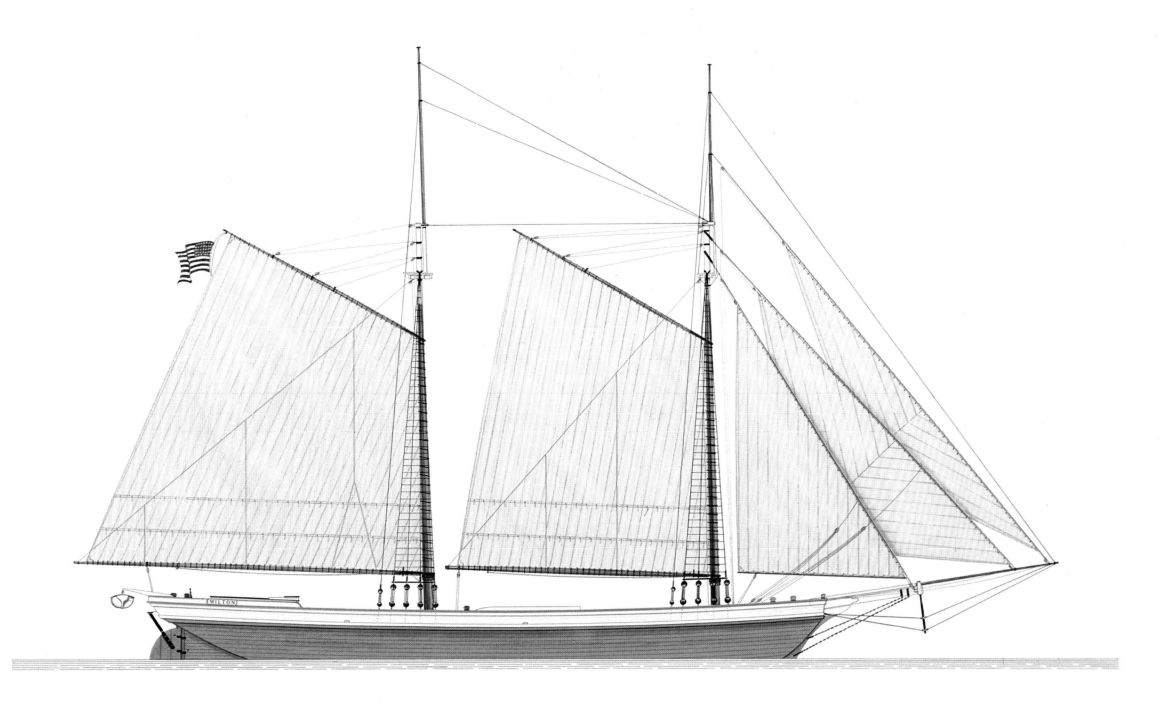

13. *Champion*   (Tug)

Because of the widespread distribution of Seth Whipple's famous lithograph, *Champion* has become the best-known of all Great Lakes tugs. She was built at Detroit in 1868 by Campbell & Owen. Her twin-cylinder high-pressure engine made her one of the most powerful tugs of her day. At 134 feet in length, with a 21.4-foot beam, and depth of 10.7 feet, she was also one of the largest. Although famous for her Detroit River tows, she also traveled to other parts of the Lakes. Thus it was that she burned while at Put-in-Bay, Ohio, on September 15, 1903.

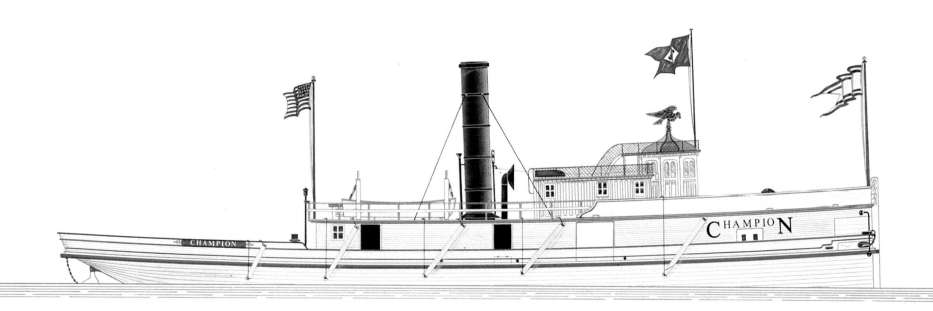

14. *Lucia A. Simpson* (Schooner)

The schooner *Lucia A. Simpson* was built of oak by Rand & Burger at Manitowoc, Wisconsin, in 1875. With a length of 127 feet, a 28-foot beam, depth of 8.7 feet, and a gross tonnage of 227, she was noted for her speed. For a wooden vessel her days were unusually long. She fitted out in 1929, but a broken spar cut short her season and she was towed to the "boneyard" at Sturgeon Bay where she lay until destroyed, along with several other retired vessels, by fire on December 5, 1935.

15. *David Dows*   (Bark)

As the only five-masted vessel ever built upon the Lakes, *David Dows* was tried with both schooner and bark rigs, but apparently neither proved successful as she spent most of her short life as a tow barge. She was built of wood with iron strapping by the Bailey Brothers at Toledo in 1881. With a length of 265.4 feet, a beam of 37.6 feet and a depth of 18.1 feet, she was a giant among Great Lakes sailing vessels and, according to several sources, the largest schooner in the world at the time of her launch. She foundered about ten miles southeast of Chicago on November 29, 1889.

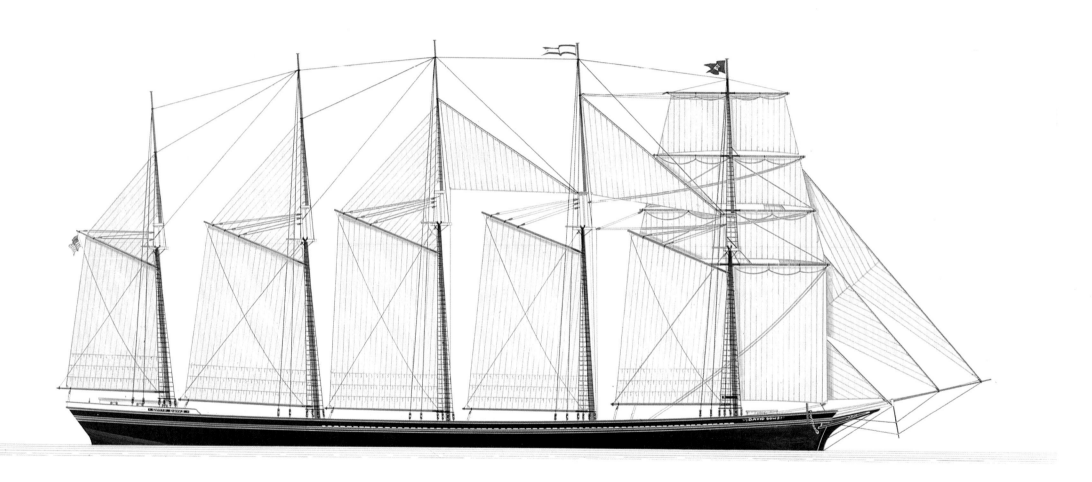

16. *Onoko* (Steamer)

The evolution of the typical Great Lakes bulk carrier with forward cabins separated from after cabins and machinery by an unbroken cargo space was a slow process with many important milestones. One of these was *Onoko* of 1882. She was the first to be built of iron and, although wooden bulk freighters continued to be built for almost twenty more years, her success spelled the eventual transition to metal hulls. With a length of 287.3 feet, 38.8-foot beam and depth of 20.7 feet, *Onoko* was the largest of her day. She lasted until 1915 when she foundered off Knife Island, Lake Superior.

17. *Lansdowne* (Car Ferry)

Even on the Great Lakes where longevity is taken for granted, *Lansdowne's* long career is noteworthy. Designed by Frank E. Kirby to utilize the engines built in 1873 for the wooden car ferry *Michigan, Lansdowne* was built of iron in 1884 by the Detroit Dry Dock Company at Wyandotte, Michigan. She is 294 feet long, with a beam of 41.3 feet and depth of 13 feet, measuring 1571 gross tons. Although sidewheelers are not usually considered good icebreakers, *Lansdowne* was an exception. She crossed the Detroit River under her own power until 1970, when one of her antique engines flew apart. Since that time she has served as a barge on the same run.

18. *Barge 101* (Whaleback Barge)

Barge 101 was Captain Alexander McDougall's first whaleback, a design he developed from years of observing vessels fight the waves of the Great Lakes. His craft permitted the seas to roll harmlessly over them. Although *Barge 101* was launched in 1888 at Duluth, Minnesota, both of her ends had been built in Brooklyn, New York. She was 191 feet in length, with a beam of 25 feet and depth of 18 feet, measuring only 428 gross tons, but she proved to be the forerunner of a large fleet of whaleback barges and steamers which became the trademark of the Great Lakes. *Barge 101* died far from the Lakes when she foundered off Seal Island, Maine, on December 3, 1908.

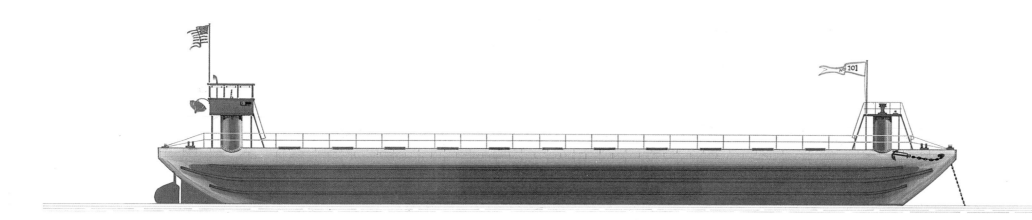

19. *Sidney O. Neff*   (Steam Barge)

In 1890 Burger & Burger built the wooden schooner-barge
Sidney O. Neff at Manitowoc, Wisconsin. She was 149.6 feet
long, with a 30.2-foot beam, and depth of 10.4 feet. Her early
years were spent as a barge on the end of a tow line, but about
1897 an engine was placed in her and she became a steamer.
The conversion was apparently successful as she continued to
serve in a variety of trades until she was abandoned for age
at Marinette, Wisconsin, in 1940. For a brief time she bore
the name *M.C. & M.C. No. 2* but this was soon changed
back to *Sidney O. Neff*.

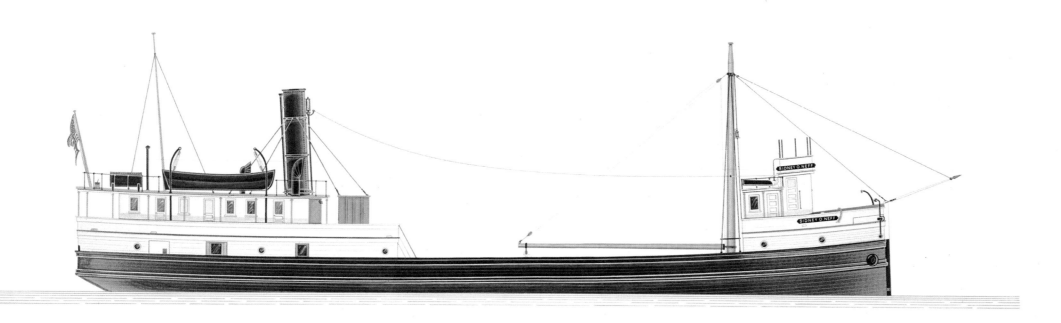

20. *Yukon*   (Schooner-Barge)

The four-masted schooner-barge *Yukon,* built at West Bay City, Michigan, by F. W. Wheeler in 1893 was one of the later and larger sailing vessels on the Lakes. Constructed of oak, she was 270 feet in length, with a 42-foot beam and a depth of 19.6 feet. Her 1602 gross ton measurement was large for her type. *Yukon* foundered off Ashtabula, Ohio, October 25, 1905.

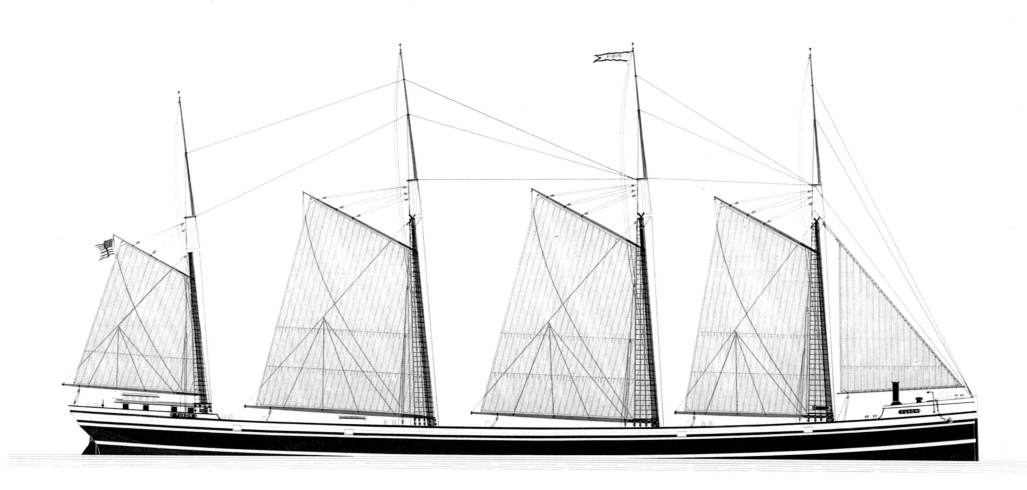

21. *John Ericsson*   (Whaleback Steamer)

The steamer *John Ericsson,* named for the inventor of the screw propeller, was the largest and the last of the true whaleback steamers. She was 390 feet in length, with a 48-foot beam, and 27-foot depth. Built in 1896, the vessel was hull 138 at the American Steel Barge Company's West Superior, Wisconsin, yard. She served long and faithfully as a bulk carrier in both American and Canadian Great Lakes fleets. Upon her retirement she almost became a marine museum, but after several plans fell through she was cut up for scrap at Hamilton, Ontario, in 1967–68. Thus to her smaller sister, *Meteor,* earlier converted to a tanker, goes the title of the last remaining whaleback. The 380-foot *Meteor* has been preserved as a museum ship at Superior, near the site of her launch.

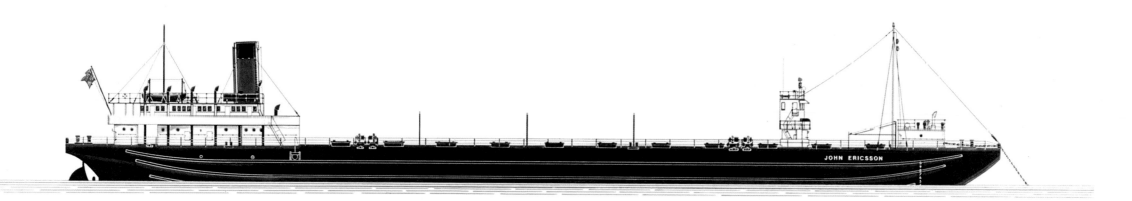

22. *Pere Marquette 18*　(Car Ferry)

Pere Marquette 18 was built in 1902 at Cleveland, Ohio, by the American Ship Building Company. With a length of 338 feet, beam of 56 feet, and depth of 19.5 feet, she was intended as a railroad car ferry for the Flint & Pere Marquette Railway's Lake Michigan service. However, during the summers she often had her car deck planked over as a dance floor and operated as a passenger excursion steamer out of Chicago. Shortly after returning from this service in September of 1910, she foundered twenty miles off Sheboygan, Wisconsin, with the loss of 38 lives. She was replaced in the railroad service by a new vessel, which was also named *Pere Marquette 18.*

23. *C. F. Bielman, Jr.* (Steamer)

C. F. Bielman, Jr. served for many years as a floating post office and mail delivery boat at Detroit. Her unusual hull design made it possible for her to "hang close" to passing vessels while delivering the mail on the move. The 67.5-foot steamer has a 14-foot beam and a depth of 7.3 feet. She was built by Johnston Brothers at Ferrysburg, Michigan, in 1907. In the mid-1930s she was sold for use as a workboat with a diesel engine replacing her steam power plant. In recent years she has been in service as a yacht at Toledo carrying the name *Dove*.

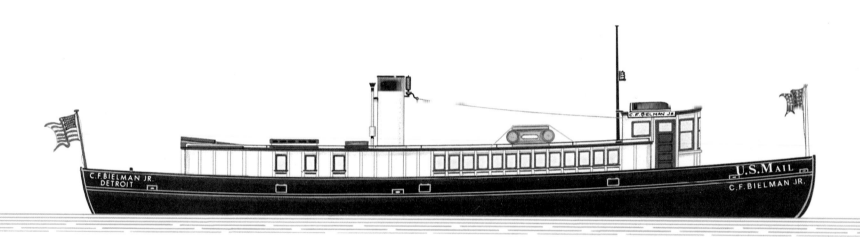

24. *Wyandotte* (Steamer)

When the Great Lakes Engineering Works launched
Wyandotte at Ecorse, Michigan, in 1908, it marked the birth
of a design that over the next 65 years was to become supreme
in Great Lakes bulk-carrying vessels. Although makeshift
self-unloading systems had been installed aboard the wooden
Hennepin in 1903, and another wooden vessel on the Lakes
and one on the Pacific Coast had subsequently been converted,
the Michigan Alkali Company's *Wyandotte* was the first
vessel to be built as a self-unloader. She was 286 feet in length,
with a beam of 45.2 feet and depth of 24 feet. A series of
conveyors made it possible for her to quickly and efficiently
unload her bulk cargoes and stack them neatly on shore
without the aid of dockside equipment. Although worthy of
preservation as a historical and technological landmark, this
venerable pioneer was scrapped at Port Colborne, Ontario,
during the winter of 1966–67.

25. *United States*   (Steamer)

Built in 1909 at Manitowoc, Wisconsin, as a day passenger steamer for service on Lake Michigan, the *United States* was originally 193 feet long, with a 41-foot beam and depth of 16 feet. She had an extremely varied career. In 1916 she was purchased by Colonel Edward Green and taken to New York City, where she was lengthened to 259 feet and rebuilt as one of the largest and most palatial yachts of her day. But the Colonel soon tired of her and 1923 found her again in New York City being reconverted to a passenger vessel. Her return to Lake Michigan was largely unsuccessful, and while tied up at Sarnia, Ontario, in 1927 she burned. Two years later she was taken to Lauzon, Quebec, rebuilt as a package freighter, and renamed *Batiscan*. She ran in the package trade only until 1931 and was laid up at various St. Lawrence river ports until she was finally scrapped at Sorel, Quebec, in 1945.

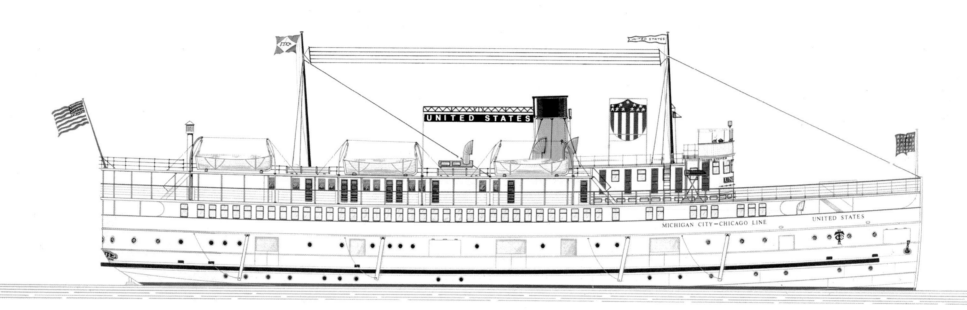

26. *Renown* (Tanker)

In 1912 *Renown* became the first self-propelled vessel to be
built on the Great Lakes for service as a tanker carrying
liquid petroleum products. The 373-foot steamer had a 52-foot
beam and a depth of 25 feet. She was built as hull 396 at
Lorain, Ohio, by the American Ship Building Company for
the Standard Transportation Company, which was then a
division of the Standard Oil Company of New York. In 1930
she was renamed *Beaumont Parks* and in 1957 she became
Mercury. She continued to ply the Lakes until sold for
scrapping in 1975.

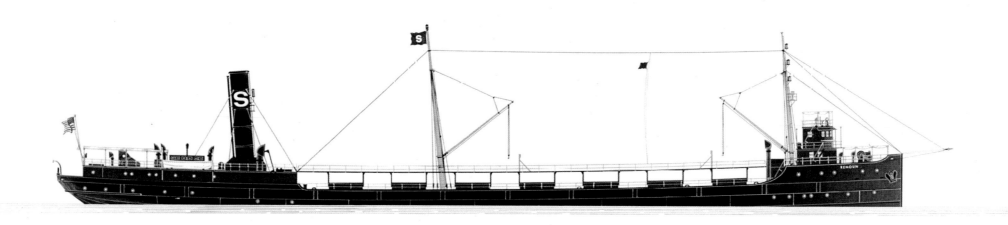

27. *South American*   (Steamer)

Although when she was built at Ecorse, Michigan, in 1914 the
South American had only one smoke stack, this veteran
passenger steamer is best remembered as having two. She
received her second stack (which is a dummy) when she was
converted to burn oil in 1922. Following a fire which gutted
her superstructure while she was docked at Holland, Michigan,
September 9, 1924, she was again rebuilt with two stacks.
She is 290.6 feet long, with a 47.1-foot beam and depth of
18.3 feet. Operated throughout her career by the Chicago,
Duluth & Georgian Bay Transit Company, the *South American*
and her nearly identical sister *North American* were familiar
sights throughout the Upper Lakes and, after its opening in
1959, along the St. Lawrence Seaway as well. Because of new
safety regulations, the *South* was sold following the 1967
season and towed to Piney Point, Maryland, for use as a
floating dormitory, a use that never materialized. As the
Bicentennial Year dawned, a group from Duluth were
attempting to rescue the *South* from a New Jersey scrapyard
and return her to the Lakes as a floating tourist attraction.

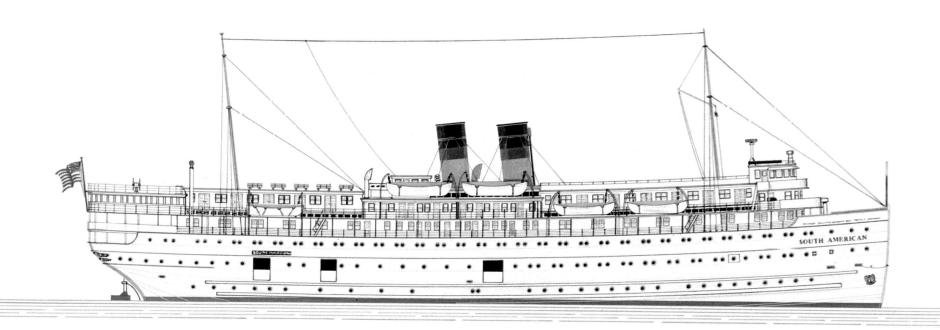

28. U. S. *Light Vessel 103*

Although built in 1920 at Morris Heights, New York, this lightship spent almost all of her days on the Great Lakes. Her stations were varied. From 1920 until 1923 she was a relief vessel; from 1924 to 1929 she was stationed at Grays Reef in the Straits of Mackinac; from 1930 to 1932 she was again a relief vessel based at Milwaukee; from 1933 until 1934 she was on Manitou station on Lake Michigan; and finally from 1935 through 1970 she was on Huron station at the extreme southern end of Lake Huron. When the U.S. Coast Guard took her over from the U.S. Lighthouse Service in 1939 she was officially renumbered WAL 526 but she was popularly known as "Huron." As built she was only 69.5 feet long, with a 24-foot beam and depth of 11 feet. She was powered by a 175-horsepower steam engine. In 1936 she was lengthened to 97 feet, and in 1949 she received a pair of diesel engines. "Huron" was the only American lightship to have a black hull. When she was retired in 1970 she was the last light vessel upon the Lakes. She is now a landlocked marine museum at Port Huron.

29. *Henry Ford II* (**Motor Vessel**)

When *Henry Ford II* and her near-sister *Benson Ford* were launched in 1924, they were the first major Lake vessels to be powered by diesel engines. Both have served faithfully ever since with their opposed cylinder Sun-Doxford engines still chugging merrily along. However, in 1974 the *Henry Ford II* was rebuilt as a self-unloader, thus giving her the probability of many more years of service. Her length is 597.5 feet, beam 62.2 feet, and depth 27.8 feet. When the elder Henry Ford was alive, he was frequently a passenger aboard *Henry Ford II,* which he had named for his grandson.

30. *Stewart J. Cort* (Motor Vessel)

When she entered service in 1972, the motor vessel *Stewart J. Cort* became by far the largest vessel ever to sail upon the Great Lakes. With a length of 1000 feet, a beam of 105 feet, and depth of 49 feet, this giant self-unloader is capable of carrying 58,000 long tons of taconite pellets and discharging them at the rate of 20,000 long tons per hour. The *Cort's* bow and stern were constructed at Pascagoula, Mississippi, and sailed into the Lakes as *Hull 1173*. At Erie, Pennsylvania, they were cut apart and joined to the midsection, which had been built by the Erie Marine Division of Litton Industries as their hull 101.

Le Griffon, 60 ft.   *Washington Monument, 550 ft.*

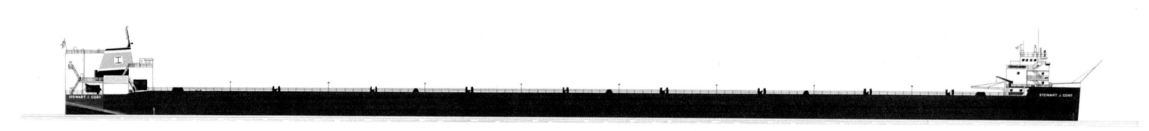

31. *Paul Thayer*   (Motor Vessel)

Paul Thayer is typical of the new breed of smaller self-unloading bulk motor vessels entering service on the Lakes in the 1970s. She was built in 1973 as hull 902 at the Lorain, Ohio, yard of the American Ship Building Company. Her 610-foot profile displays the modern, cabins-aft, squared-off lines that are now becoming common on the Lakes. Her other dimensions are beam 68 feet, depth 36.9 feet. She is currently operated by the Pringle Transit Company and sports the "P-ring-gull" stack marking made famous on the Lakes by the old Pringle Barge Line.

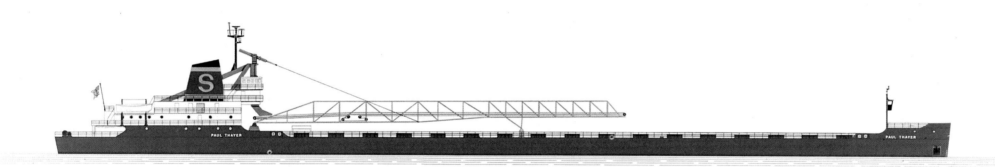

As a Bicentennial project, the Detroit Historical Society Guild
commissioned Detroit artist Karl Kuttruff to undertake the thirty-one
paintings included in this volume, representing two hundred
years of navigation on the Great Lakes.

A product designer by profession, Kuttruff enjoys building
ship models and had been producing his acrylic paintings of ships—
using brush, ruling pen, and airbrush—since 1969. His "vessel
broadsides" have been exhibited at the Dossin Great Lakes Museum
(1972) and the State Historical Museum in Lansing (1974).

To achieve historical accuracy in dimension and color, Kuttruff
studied actual shipyard drawings, old photographs, government
records, and newspaper accounts. He also gleaned valuable
information from interviews with old-timers on the Lakes.

Robert E. Lee is curator of the Dossin Great Lakes Museum,
coordinating director of the Great Lakes Maritime Institute, and
editor of *Telescope* magazine. His professional and civic interests
include the Propeller Club of the United States–Port of Detroit,
Algonquin Club, International Shipmasters Association, Historical
Society of Michigan, and the Detroit Historical Society.

David T. Glick is assistant to the director of education and
manager of adult education, Henry Ford Museum.

The book is designed by Richard Kinney. The type is Linotype
Caledonia for the text and Caslon Old Style for display. The
paper is S. D. Warren's Patina and the book is bound in
Columbia Mills Fictionette cloth over boards. Manufactured in the
United States of America.